some recent snowflakes
(and other things)

some recent snowf

1979
printed editions
new york, ny and west glover, vt

kes

(and other things)

by dick higgins

isbn: 0–914162–36–5 (cloth edition)
isbn: 0–914162–37–3 (paper edition)

contents: snowflakes

contents: other things

some recent snowflakes

snowflake: which shines brighter?

<pre>
the idea of gold
                or
          gold
                or
          gold   itself
                or
                   itself
                or
the idea
                or
the idea
           of
the idea
                or
the idea

                or
                   itself
                or
          gold   itself
                or
          gold
                or
the idea of gold
</pre>

asolo
august 28, 1977

9

from 1959/60: lyrical text #13

                    together
                    alone
               to be
desire
               to be alone
               to be together
desire
                    watching
desire
               to be together
               to be alone
desire
               to be
                         alone
                         together

west glover
july, 1978

eight year snowflake (for e.w.)

time
        butterfly
monarch
        of the summer
monarch
        butterfly
    time
        for it to die
      end
        time
monarch
        butterfly
monarch
        of the summer
      time
        for it to die
monarch
        butterfly
        end
        for them

end
    butterfly
end
    of the summer
end
    butterfly
end
    for them
end
    butterfly
monarch
    for it to die
  time
    of the summer
monarch
    butterfly
monarch
    time
  end
    for it to die
  time
    butterfly
monarch
    of the summer
monarch
    butterfly
  time

new york
30. x. 78

snowflake: on turning forty

        raging
            on ahead
    time's
        raging on ahead
  of
    time's
    time
  of time's raging
          ahead
  of time's raging
about time
      desolate
about time
  of time's raging
         ahead
  of time's raging
    time
    time's
  of
        raging on ahead
    time's
          on ahead
        raging

             new york
           january 29, 1978

a snowflake on may 5th

the bread
the art
that's baked
art
that happens
bread
that's baked
bread
that happens
and thee
that happens
bread
that's baked
bread
that happens
art
that's baked
the art
the bread

nyc
may 5th, 1978

flight from italy, a snowflake

<pre>
                    earths flowers dreams
                dreams earths flowers
            flowers dreams earths
earths flowers dreams
day to be born
    to be born *night*
day to be born
day
                night   (natura morta $\stackrel{?}{=}$ still life)
day
day to be born
    to be born *night*
day to be born
earths flowers dreams
        flowers dreams earths
            dreams earths flowers
            earths flowers dreams
</pre>

cavriago, italy
18 august, 1977

two swedish snowflakes for mats b

het
syskon
hetero
syskonhet
kon
ero ti
kon
syskonhet
hetero
syskon
het

16

<pre>
          gen
        rogen
              vinner
        trogen
               kvinnar
        trogen
               vinner
               vinner
        rogen
          gen
</pre>

milwaukee
14 may, 1977

le tombeau de françois villon

ris
ris
ris
ris
ris
ris
ris
ris
ris
ris
ris
cris
écris
cris
ris
ris
ris
ris
ris
ris
ris
ris
ris
ris
ris

new york
12 iii 76

18

the lord's bad penny
i am
keep turning up
i am
that
i am
keep turning up
i am
the lord's bad penny
i am
keep turning up
i am
that
i am
keep turning up
i am
the lord's bad penny
i am
keep turning up
i am
that
i am
keep turning up
i am
the lord's bad penny
i am
keep turning up
i am
that
i am
keep turning up
i am
the lord's bad penny
i am
keep turning up
i am
that
i am
keep turning up
i am
the lord's bad penny
i am

caryatid: i am

(to be written upon the air
and strung from the bottom
of the sea to the top of the
moon)

new york city
6 november, 1977

premonitions

the empty cup
contains
the empty cup

and the word?

new york
18 february, 1978

double snowflake: dilemma

i

like
i only
like you
but
like
but
i give
curries and
stars   and
cheeses and
mountains   and
i
only
like you but
only
i
mountains   and
cheeses and
stars   and
curries and

i give
but
  like
but
  like you
i only
  like

                  ii

    love
i   you
i give
        sweet
i   sweet
i   apple pie
   only sweet apple pie
                    apple pie
   only
i
   only
                    apple pie
   only sweet apple pie
                    apple pie
i
i   sweet
        sweet
i give
i   you
   love

                              west glover, vt
                         16 september, 1978

half a snowflake

look
is it dark or
look

       or
look through your life
at

       through your life
at your shadow—
is it dark

       or
does it glow

       or
is it dark
at your shadow—

     through your life
at
look through your life

       or
look
look
is it dark or
look

nyc
7 may 1978

from 1959/60: lyrical text #12

<pre>
        hardly
  i can   tell who they are
  i can hardly tell who they are
    can
  i
                tell
                    who   are
                        they
                    who they are
                        they
                    who   are
                tell
  i
    can
        hardly
  i can hardly tell who they are
  i can   tell who they are
        hardly
</pre>

west glover, vt
july, 1978

life on his wife's casting couch

polishing remains
remains polishing
the
polishing the remains
remains
polishing the remains
the
remains polishing
polishing remains

of
an act of being
being
an act
of
an act
being
an act of being
of

milwaukee
2 june, 1977

26

february snowflake

frost and *fire*
frost

                    of
            fire
life   of
    frost and
life

                    of
            fire
life
    within
life
    frost   of
                    someone who left
            and *fire* of
                    his memory
            and *fire* of
                    someone who left
    frost   of
life
    within
life

27

fire
of
life
frost and
life
of
fire
of
frost
frost and *fire*

buffalo, ny
february 18, 1979

snowflake: man's heart's mirror's

<pre>
                        man's heart's mirror's
                mirror's man's heart's
        heart's mirror's man's
man's heart's mirror's
yes child
yes child very well
        very well i love you
                i love you yes child
        very well i love you
yes child very well
yes child
man's heart's mirror's
        heart's mirror's man's
                mirror's man's heart's
                man's heart's mirror's
</pre>

new york city
june 14, 1977

snowflake for ray johnson

                        art's ray's brother's
                brother's art's ray's
            ray's brother's art's
    art's ray's brother's
            ray's
    art's
            ray's   art's ray's
                                 art's ray's
            ray's   ray's
                                 art's ray's
            ray's   art's ray's
    art's
            ray's
    art's ray's brother's
            ray's brother's art's
                brother's art's ray's
                    art's ray's brother's

                                    new york
                                    16 october 1977
                                    happy birthday

30

two snowflakes with faces in them

                    i
                         he is
                    very poor
                         all he has
                              is
                                   money
                         it has
          separated him from his son
                         he has
                    forgotten
                              his songs
     why?
                              his songs
                    forgotten
                         he has
          separated him from his son
                         it has
                              money
                         is
                    all he has
                    very poor
                         he is

ii

very rich
  she is
  she knows many songs
     many songs
  she knows
very rich
     many songs
very rich
  she is
her children feel close to her
  she is
very rich
     many songs
very rich
  she knows
     many songs
  she knows many songs
  she is
very rich

new york
5 february, 1978

snowflake for a friend who went completely straight

                    hoop-la!
                        your beauty
                she took
                        your poetry
            she sucked out
                        your madness
                she purged
            for she said
                she'd take your child
            and
                now you are *hollow*—
                    you call yourself a warrior
            but
                    who needs *hollow* men?
                she'll leave you
                            hollow
                she'll leave you
                    who needs *hollow* men?
            but
                        you call yourself a warrior
                    now you are *hollow*—

and
    she'd take your child
for she said
    she purged
        your madness
she sucked out
        your poetry
   she took
        your beauty
     hoop-la!

                new york city
           19 november, 1978

the fnowflakes of giordano bruno

"choofing MIND to fee"

i

the   things
the little things
                woo'd
                woo'd by form
                            form
                      by
                            form
the little things woo'd
                            form
                      by
          little   form
                      by
                      great
                                  choofing
                      great
                      by
          little   form

35

                        by
                              form
the little things woo'd
                              form
                        by
                              form
                  woo'd by form
                  woo'd
the little things
the   things

ii

and

                            IS

    the river
    the billion drops of water?
and all
    the movement between the ſhores?
and all and all
    the place where terrence drowned?
and all and all and all
    the billion
and
    the place
and
    the movement
    the river

                         THE MIND'S EYE
                                'S
                        THE   EYE
                                'S
                    MIND
                          'S
                      THE   EYE
                                'S
                      THE MIND'S EYE

    the river
    the movement

and
    the place
and
    the billion
and all and all and all
    the place where terrence drowned?
and all and all
    the movement between the fhores?
and all
    the billion drops of water
    the river
              IS

and

iii

to ſee
   to ſee   the largeneſs
and to be like the largeneſs
   to be like the ſmallneſs
         like
         the largeneſs
         like
         the ſmallneſs
         like
   to   like the largeneſs
         the ſmallneſs
   to ſee
         each ſpinning world
  in its own
and infinite
   infinite ſpinning
         acting in harmony with the vaſt
   to ſee
         acting in harmony with the vaſt
   infinite ſpinning
and infinite
   in its own
         each ſpinning world
   to ſee
         the ſmallneſs

<pre>
to   like the largeneſs
        like
                the ſmallneſs
        like
                the largeneſs
        like
to be   like the ſmallneſs
and to be like the largeneſs
    to ſee   the largeneſs
    to ſee
</pre>

october 23rd, 1977
new york

the morning songs of jordan brown

i- heroic frenzy

the stream
the river
the sea
the ice
the walrus
the bonfire
the wind

a stream and the stream
a river and the river
a sea and the sea
some ice and the ice
a walrus and the walrus
a bonfire and the bonfire
a wind and the wind

watching the stream
   i am the stream
watching the river
   i am the river
watching the sea
   i am the sea
watching the ice
   i am the ice
watching the walrus
   i am the walrus
watching the bonfire
   i am the bonfire
watching the wind
   i am the wind

for the earth spreads out
from stream and river
from sea and ice
from walrus and bonfire and wind

      time
beyond it all—daytime
time to get a move on
beyond it all—daytime
      time

ii–unity of diversity

                isnt
ham isnt onions
                isnt
                                both
        but westerns need
                                both
        but
                isnt   both
        but
ham   onions   both
        but
                isnt   both
        but
                                both
        but westerns need
                                both
            isnt
ham isnt onions
            isnt

iii–relatively perceived

tension
on
tension
intension
ontension
intention
ex
sparks
from the eye
to the star
to the world
to its reflection
to the thing
behind the thing
sparks
intention   one will
sparks
behind the thing
to the thing
to its reflection
to the world
to the star

from the eye
sparks
ex
intention
ontension
intension
tension
on
tension

iv–infinitely

```
            becomes
the stream                                  infinitely
            becomes                          infinitely
  stream                                     infinitely
            becomes                          infinitely
  walrus                                     infinitely
            becomes                          infinitely
the ice                                      infinitely
            becomes                          infinitely
                   i am
  bonfire          i am                      infinitely
  wind             i am                      infinitely
  sea              i am                      infinitely
                   i am
  sea              i am                      infinitely
  wind             i am                      infinitely
  bonfire          i am                      infinitely
                   i am
```

>   becomes   infinitely
> the ice   infinitely
>   becomes   infinitely
>   walrus   infinitely
>   becomes   infinitely
>   stream   infinitely
>   becomes   infinitely
> the stream   infinitely
>   becomes

> new york
> 3 december, 1977

snowflake: dark room, dark rose

        dark
          is
          it
        dark room
        dark rose
what color?
        dark rose
               a
        dark room
            in a
              sleeping
          is
          it
what color?
          it
          is
              sleeping
            in a
        dark room
               a
        dark rose
what color?
        dark rose
        dark room
          it
          is
        dark

nyc
20.iv.78

other things

(for performing, translating and
transmuting into your own experience or
subsumptions)

long tail for jessie

once upon a time there was a kangaroo—

and that kangaroo loved another kangaroo
  and that kangaroo loved another kangaroo
    and that kangaroo loved another kangaroo
      and that kangaroo loved another kangaroo
        and that kangaroo loved another kangaroo
          and that kangaroo loved another kangaroo
            and that kangaroo loved another kangaroo
              and that kangaroo loved another kangaroo
                and that kangaroo loved another kangaroo

—which is how it sometimes goes
in kangaroo land.

new york
october 1978

glides

right right
wood wood
  yes yes
    true true
     blue blue
       swash swash
         good good
        pale pale
       hush hush
      tall tall
      tale tale
     told told
     ever ever
    north north
    button button
    baby baby
   round round
   speed speed
  slim slim
 bottom bottom
delicious delicious

new york
15 september, 1977

for several

once there was a yes
who married a 3
but 7 was cruel to them
and they had no 5

so they went to s
a land with many f's and b's
and there they lived in a big 6
happily ever after, dancing the h and the p
and eating delicious 9's

lidingö, sweden
july 25th, 1977

being in a corner of a corner of a corner of a . . .

on a 1
for a 3
with the 5
in the 5
in a 6
on the grass
with the 3
through the 6
for the 2
for a 3
in a 6
in a 4

on a 2
for a 4
with the 3
in a 1
for a 3
for the 6
in a 5
on the 5
for the 2
for a 6
on a 2
in a 3

grass
maiden
flower
province
hair
comb

rome
29.vii.77

paraSITism

an EITHER   MAN with
a nEITHER woMAN—
: why not let those horses loose?

new york
10 december, 1977

twenty
(an erotic epithalamium for george and billie maciunas)

ſeated in a red suit
twenty gong ſtrokes
it riſes
it riſes
it riſes
it riſes
it riſes
it riſes
it riſes
it riſes
it riſes
it riſes
it ſubſides
it ſubſides
it ſubſides
it ſubſides
it ſubſides
it ſubſides
it ſubſides
it ſubſides
it ſubſides
it ſubſides

25 february, 1978
new york city

cinq petits chansons populaires

(contre les –ismes, les –istes et les ismistes)
dédickés avec mes respirations les plus profondes aux
troglatydes aimables, g. brecht & r. filliou

i

l'avare aveugle
l'avare a veugles
　　veugles qui se rempent
　　　(je me trompe)
elle a de meubles
elle ache de meubles
　　meubles qui se rompent
　　　(je me trempe)
　　　ce n'est qu'un petit soreil

l'avare à meubles
l'avare ameuble
　　ameuble comme les toutes
　　　(j'ai des moûts)
elle aime les ables
elle est aimable
　　aimable comme les toutes
　　　(j'ai mes doutes)
　　　ce n'est qu'un petit soreil

58

ii

nous épillons vingt ou trente
viandes de viandes
tous habillés par de blondes
à la mode des– vous m'entendez!–
tous habillés par de blondes
à la mode de viandes

ma première valérie
que je fume à cause de ce vie
c'est d'être goupouillisé
à la mode de– vous m'entendiez!–
ma femme fumée et surbrisée
à la mode des goupouillisés

la séconde j'entrais dans sa chambre
piques alors! il s'agit du membre
j'y me murais donc sept milles écus
à la mode de– vous m'entendiez!–
d'huille peut on ne se sans bourreuilléçus
se de la mode en apperçus

la troisième j'entrais dans sa chambre
je m'en buvais de quoix en quoi?
de robiresses et séchiresses
à la mode de– vous m'entendiez!–
chaque sourire a sa maîtresse
je m'en doute des déchiresses

elle m'y a porté comme viande
à la foire de la joliejolie hollande
elle m'a vendé bon marché
et dis donc alors– vous m'entendez!–
elle m'a vendé bon marché
à une bouchière bien séchiressée

elle m'a jugé à pendre
a! je suis dur! mais de prendre
à pendre et sans se lever
mais moi quoi ben– vous m'entendez!–
à pendre et sans se lever
je m'y en poupe les poppes pour m'en reveiller

iii–le froid se peurt
(d'apres andré major)

les peaux troubles de mes désirs
les peaux fortes de mes passions
les peaux colorées de mes plaisirs
les peaux puantes de mes douleurs
les peaux tristes de ma solitude

sonnez sonnez sonnez sonnez
sonnez sonnez sonnez sonnez
sonnez les baches
sonnez les beches
sonnez les biches
sonnez les boches
sonnez les buches
sonnez sonnez sonnez sonnez
sonnez sonnez sonnez sonnez

les peaux marrantes de ma fatigue
les peaux silencieuses de mon sommeil
les peaux déchaînées de ma colère
les peaux bienfaisantes de ma joie
les peaux mystérieuses de ma vie
les peaux inconnues de la morte

sonnez sonnez sonnez sonnez
sonnez sonnez sonnez sonnez
           sonnez les baches
           sonnez les beches
           sonnez les biches
           sonnez les boches
           sonnez les buches
sonnez sonnez sonnez sonnez
sonnez sonnez sonnez sonnez

sans nez!

iv–boho bill

boho bill
vivera still
    pour le weekend
boho bill
cheveux de saintes huiles
    pour le weekend

non, ce n'est les nezes
non, ce n'est pas la neige
ou sent-on les flairs des neiges passés?
non, ce n'est pas les neiges
non, ce n'est pas le nez
y a-t-il un flair d'un negre qui se passe?
                  raciste!
                  bassiste!
                  de mentionner un nom
                  c'est d'insulter le sang!

boho bill
vivera still
    pour le weekend
boho bill
cheveaux de saintes huiles
    pour le weekend

v–hello, serbes-marines
(traduction anticlimactique du chanson célèbré du groupe
roc "les coléoptères")

inde! daounes! guerre! aivasse! borne!
l'ivre d'un mâne, ou sait le d'ainsi.
anti d'hôle, d'ours, office l'aïf!
anti-lande! serbes-marines!
heul huille, seul d'entre de sonnes—
tel huille, font d'asie afkarinne,
en d'huille, lifby! nice d'ou huève
innez—hello? serbes-marines?

refrain:
oui, olive de nez—
hello, serbes-marines!
et   hello, serbes-marines!
et   hello, serbes-marines!
oui, olive de nez—
hello, serbes-marines!
et   hello, serbes-marines!
et   hello, serbes-marines!

entre heures, furendes huêres à la borde,
    m'en y mort, afdamme, l'ivre n'extort,
    en de débande, beguinne de plaït!

refrain:
    "oui, olive de nez" (etc.)

veule estime à hatte! mystère! capitaine!
    garotte à quippe et d'y venne.

refrain:
    "oui, olive de nez" (etc.)

en d'huille. l'ivre a l'aïf office,
    avar y en à face—hasse à lui nitte—
ce quai a fait bleu, ou entre ces effets grinnes—
    en heure—hello, serbes-marines!

refrain:
    "oui, olive de nez" (etc.)

west glover, vt
october, 1974

proteus's campfire

his lay lady lay
his lady lay lay
lay his lay lady
lay his lady lay
lady his lay lay
lay lay his lady
lay lady his lay
lady lay his lay
lay lay lady his
lay lady lay his
lady lay lay his
his lay lay lady

his love lady lay
his love lay lady
his lady love lay
his lady lay love
his lay love lady
his lay lady love
love his lady lay
love his lay lady
love lady his lay
love lady lay his
love lay his lady

love lay lady his
lady his love lay
lady his lay love
lady love his lay
lady love lay his
lady lay his love
lady lay love his
lay his love lady
lay his lady love
lay love his lady
lay love lady his
lay lady his love
lay lady love his

lady lob by the fire
lady by the fire lob
lob lady by the fire
lob by the fire lady
by the fire lady lob
by the fire lob lady

lady love by the fire
lady by the fire love
love lady by the fire
love by the fire lady
by the fire lady love
by the fire love lady

love high love low
love high low love
love low love high
love low high love
high love love low
high love low love
high low love love
low love love high
low love high love
low high love love
love love high low
love love low high

love hard love slow
love hard slow love
love slow love hard
love slow hard love
hard love love slow
hard love slow love
hard slow love love
slow love love hard
slow love hard love
slow hard love love
love love hard slow
love love slow hard

lob lady lay by the fire
lob lady by the fire lay
lob lay lady by the fire
lob lay by the fire lady
lob by the fire lady lay
lob by the fire lay lady
lady lob lay by the fire
lady lob by the fire lay
lady lay lob by the fire
lady lay by the fire lob
lady by the fire lob lay
lady by the fire lay lob
lay lob lady by the fire
lay lob by the fire lady
lay lady lob by the fire
lay lady by the fire lob
lay by the fire lob lady
lay by the fire lady lob
by the fire lob lady lay
by the fire lob lay lady
by the fire lady lob lay
by the fire lady lay lob
by the fire lay lob lady
by the fire lay lady lob

love lady lay by the fire
love lady by the fire lay
love lay lady by the fire
love lay by the fire lady
love by the fire lady lay
love by the fire lay lady
lady love lay by the fire
lady love by the fire lay
lady lay love by the fire
lady lay by the fire love
lady by the fire love lay
lady by the fire lay love
lay love lady by the fire
lay love by the fire lady
lay lady love by the fire
lay lady by the fire love
lay by the fire love lady
lay by the fire lady love
by the fire love lady lay
by the fire love lay lady
by the fire lady love lay
by the fire lady lay love
by the fire lay love lady
by the fire lay lady love

new york city
may 7, 1979

Piece for Meredith Monk's Apartment

1., Naked except for a night gown, rain coat or other light covering. Blindfolded.

2., Starting from the left-hand wall of the kitchen, feeling one's way around the kitchen and out of it, along the wall by the bedroom, up steps, down into the bedroom, around and out of the bedroom, past windows and bookcases, down the steps, past the record player and out of the apartment area, into and all the way around the studio back to the point where one began. Identifying silently to oneself each object one encounters, as one feels one's way along.

3., Any number of people involved, but no one close to the person ahead or behind.

Generalized procedure: following the outer walls of *any* space using the process described above, identifying objects encountered, etc.

November 26th, 1968
New York City

Circle for a Few Friends

1., Five or more couples, arranged boy, girl, boy, girl, etc.

2., The couples form a circle, facing outwards, hands joined. The chair is behind one participant.

3., The circle moves to the left, so that the chair is behind each participant in turn. The participant sits down and stands up again; no matter how slowly the standing and sitting occur, the participant does not remain seated for any significant amount of time.

4., The overall duration is free, as is the number of times the circle revolves.

5., Two ideal versions: the performers naked under overcoats, wearing blinder masks made of aluminum foil. Or even better: the event takes place on a warm, sunny day on a huge lawn, with many many participants, all nude—and the performance lasts several hours, silently proceeding on and on and on.

New York
December 14, 1968

staying put

of one
is two
and so
is yes
and if
and so
& four
& more
but if
yet no
or six
me not
in yon
der if
fly up
my yes
he did
did he

nyc
11.iii.78

73

meta-

he was religious about religion
and arty about art
and natural about nature
and absurd about absurdity
and wordy about words
and neurotic about neurosis
and strong about strength
and objective about objectivity
and caring about cares
and bitter about bitterness
and loving about lovers.

he was sweet to the sweet
and nasty to the nasty
and friendly to the friendly
and manly to the manly
and kindly to the kindly
and silly to the silly
and loving to the loving.

he fooled with foolishness
and laughed about laughter
and hated to hate
and raged about raging
and believed in belief
and avoided avoiding
and studied studying
and trusted in trust
and loved to be loved.

but was he cowardly to cowards
or disturbed by disturbance?
or comic about comedy?
or womanly to women?
or musical about music?
or disastrous about disaster?
or smelly about smells?
well, he loved to make love.

so he kidded the kidders
and kissed the kissers
and punched the punchers
and pulled the pullers
and dreamed to dream
and hoped to hope
and regretted to regret
and ate with the eaters
and sported with the sports
and sang to sing
and whirled to whirl
and ducked to duck
and pretended to pretend
and intended to intend
and
and
and loved to love.

new york
20 october, 1977

Twelve Telephone Translations (for Steve McCaffery)

First Telephone Translation:
from Daniel Nabarowski (1573–1640)

Pochodnie, gwiazdy, słońca, nieba i bogowie.
Poor Charlie's done ya—give ya odds the slow kneeds
            're no better than the bogey's.
Four chairs're down there. If it grieves you,
            see *Thessalonians*. We're better at the boogey.
For chores, cars're done here. Reprieved, your kettle's
            lonely. Let her at the bugs.
The chorus scars a dunce. Believe
            hospitals only. Leaden mugs.
You're poor, so curse and dance. Grief's only
            for the bony. Let them hug.
Your porch is tarred and done. Reprieve a little
            loneliness. Leave off your duds.
Tour with Port Chester's bums. (
). For men are clods.
The torches, stars, suns, firmaments and gods.

Second Telephone Translation:
from Andreas Gryphius (1616–1664)

Nacht lichter als der Tag! Nacht, mehr denn lichte Nacht!
Naked. Liked her as they dug! Naked, merely down like naked!
Snaked, lighter as they dig! Snaked; here we drown my snake!
Make it light. Hera's shady. Make it. Heros crown my wake.
Shake it, lighters shake away. Shake it, tyros on the make.
Take, eat. Light us. Run away. Take, eat. Pour the rest away.
Might, fight? Light us on our way. Might fight? Let's go right away.
Might? Light us like the day. Might? That's right, it's bright.
Night, lighter than the day! Night, more then light, the night!

Third Telephone Translation:
from Ignjat Djordjić (1676–1737)

Prid tvo'em zlatom zlato krije;
Pride took 'em, slapped 'em. Silly though to cry.
Writing some crap then. Sally couldn't try;
Height by the crap then. Billy's sure to pry.
Hit for their brass I am. I'm sure to fold;
But for their past I'd be old.
Before he told me I'd be cold;
But for the cold of you I'd be bold,—
Before the gold of you hides gold.

Fourth Telephone Translation:
from Jean de la Ceppède (1550?–1622)

Ce nectar, par qui seul le monde est rachetable—
See nectar. Parakeets assailing lemons? That's regrettable.
Say "nectar." A pair o' kids sailing lemons that are wettable.
So—nectar. Appalled by kites, she moans that we're not able.
But nectar. And Paul hikes, and she bemoans how we're incapable.
Yes nectar. The bitch! Yikes—it's known she's crazable.
Yet nectar. My bitch and bone unfurled—it's risible.
Sweet nectar. Why bitch or moan when she's curled and praisable?
That nectar, by which alone the world is savable.

Fifth Telephone Translation:
from Adam Michna of Otravice (ca. 1600–1676)

Dým v povětři větrem hyne,—
Dumb in the poverty of vesper hymns,
And then is the poetry of whispers thin.
Amen to the cloak of whimpers and coughs—
I'm into the croak and the winter's cross.
Disinterred by the brook, all my winterwear goes off—
We're for the stroke and enough to ward ills off,
We're smoke and rough winds bear us off.

Sixth Telephone Translation:
from Giordano Bruno (1548–1600)

En velut in sacrae speciem te extollere mentis—
Envelopes are a sacred species, he tries to tell the mantis.
And mellow as a rakish priest he prays they'll document his.
He must. It's a maukish point. He craves they'll brew some,
But trusts that in his mind's the point. He's brave, they're gruesome.
Some crusts that we could find, the might that's right,—
                                        I've prayed they're true.
The lusts in which I wind, they brighten. Kindly braise a few.
Sallust has intertwined the might of wind and cravings for a view,—
See, just as in the kind of rite of mind I've praised to you.

Seventh Telephone Translation:
from Constantijn Huygens (1596–1687)

Ondanckbaerlik verspilt, verspeelt, verspelt in Son-dagh—
Unthink bears! Look,—we're split, we're spoiled,
                                        we're spooled at sun-down
And thankless and shook. We're spent, we're bent,
                                        we're fooled downtown,
And pointless books are smacked and cracked and stacked around us.
But reckless crooks are hailed and hurled and foiled each Monday,
A baleful look is given, taken, understood on Wednesday—
And we?
Ungrateful—spoiled, spilled, spelled as Sin-day.

Eighth Telephone Translation:
from Luís de Camões (1524–1580)

Mudam-se os tempos, mudam-se as vontades—
Oh madam's got her times, and madam has her wishes.
And madam's got her tympani—madam has false teeth.
And my dame's got a simple one while I'm at the Grange.
The time's nearly done, and the will has its range.
The timekeeper changes, and my will's not arranged.
The times change, the rocks and rills change.
For time is change, and rock and roll will change,
And I'll change, and you will change.
The times change, the wills change.

Ninth Telephone Translation:
from Mikhail Vassilevich Lomonosov (1711–1765)

Tam sporit zhirna mgla s vodoy—
Tom's split on an ear-knob, mangling his head—oy!
Tom's spirit's a weird one, dangling and dead—oy!
And his eye is feared. Jangling he said—"Oy!"
And his cry was heard. In an inkling I said—"Oy!"
And I tried to avoid hearing, with darkling dread—"Oy!"
As his bride and his daughter cradled him there—oy!—
It was not as it ought to be, calm around there—oy!
Dense fog and water quarrel there.

Tenth Telephone Translation:
from Giovanni Leone Sempronio (1603–1646)

Oh Dio, che cosa è l'uom? L'uom è pittura.
Oh Diane, what's the cause of ailing? Whom do we pitch to?
Ah Diane, inside's the cause. Rebellion, if true, is depicted.
Hmm. Diane, if a bride's got gauze and it's smelly,
                                    how cruel to be afflicted.
Yes, Diane, I've tried to get lost. But I tell you, I feel rejected.
No, Diane. Broadly speaking I smell you and feel dejected.
Yes, broadly thus I am, and you bellow, then you lecture.
"No, broad is what I am. That's no conjecture."
Oh Lord, what's a man? A man's a picture.

Eleventh Telephone Translation:
from Ann Bradstreet (1612–1672)

The season's now at hand of all and each,
And reason's my command. I've balled with the rich,
Now I've lightened my demand. Controlled by the bitch
I've crossed the Rio Grande, upheld the laws, and stitched
My gross of rubber bands into robes. I've switched
The decent underhand, and, well, it's such a
Recent undertaking to crawl on the beach—
The season's now at hand of all and each.

Twelfth Telephone Translation:
from Lope de Vega (1562–1635)

Desmayarse, atraverse, estar furioso.
That's my arse that you're traversing, furious star.
But if that's ever what you rehearse, that's fine for us.
And if you're painted like a hearse, like mine for instance,
Well, I'd constrain you to be light—that's in the dance.
Hell, that's paint. But in the light it's sheer brilliance.
Restraint is not for Brent, nor he for us.
Fall faint, be insolent or be furious.

New York City
June 4, 1978

a paschal poem

the heart has its reasons which the mind doesn't know,
and if you push, if you touch, they may or may not show.
to persist and then to desist—it's too much for just one night,
aristocrats and workers alike crave the strong light.
mellow men love best, and the brave ones can forgive:
weaker ones will wander and will crave to be alive.
winsome on the caper, we should brew a paper child,
but i'd rather never rape her—such a force is never mild.
embossed on blue paper there are twenty yet to try
the cross of night rantings, stars glued to the sky.
behind the madonna's gentlest ligature—
in the oldest corner of the oldest picture

we must think—we must do—in bitterest brine.
a frosted breast for a shower, a box that's divine—
you'd caress its hard flower and cherish its wine.
if you had a tower to twist and entwine—
she's loved and she's listened, she's lost and she's balled,
secure in her bower of noses enthralled.
but a shower of blood roses like gauls who still live
have an ale, love—my mood's thick and nothing could give,
entwined and unwinding, thrice crowned and twice pinned—
let a frail air of music blow thin through the wind.
then the heart of my reason unwinds in the snow;
if a cart and a bison might roll to bordeaux,
there's an art for all seasons which a kind man should show:
the heart has its reasons which the mind doesn't know.

the heart has its reasons which the mind doesn't know;
there's an art for all seasons which a kind man should show:
if a cart and a bison might roll to bordeaux,
then the heart of my reason unwinds in the snow.
let a frail air of music blow thin through the wind,
entwined and unwinding, thrice crowned and twice pinned—
have an ale, love—my mood's thick and nothing could give
but a shower of blood roses like gauls who still live.
secure in her bower of noses enthralled,
she's loved and she's listened, she's lost and she's balled.
if you had a tower to twist and entwine
you'd caress its hard flower and cherish its wine.
a frosted breast for a shower, a box that's divine—
we must think—we must do—in bitterest brine.
in the oldest corner of the oldest picture,

behind the madonna's gentlest ligature—
the cross of night rantings, stars glued to the sky,
embossed on blue paper there are twenty yet to try.
but i'd rather never rape her—such a force is never mild,
winsome on the caper, we should brew a paper child.
weaker ones will wander and will crave to be alive;
mellow men love best, and the brave ones can forgive.
aristocrats and workers alike crave the strong light—
to persist and then to desist—it's too much for just one night.
and if you push, if you touch, they may or may not show
the heart has its reasons which the mind doesn't know.

new york city
25 february, 1979

The Truth about Sadie Mee

A tangle of thoughts—a hit and a hangle, a spinning mind's spangle, and here is an angle: oh Sadie Mee (yessiree, yessiree)— the new gal in town. Oh to make a paunchy whaunchy on our, well, forget it.

This thing and that thing, this truth and that truth, oh what's the difference! "Come," you said, "if you want to." But did I think about it? I can scarce remember.

I told you I didn't want any of those while I was doing these, but you brought me those and I forgot I hadn't needed any—just such a that. A that. Yes, a this and a that.

And, Lord!—what a delicately formed chin. And on you was—yes, they were threads, as threads mean threads, slangy and kinda casual like. I've heard of a fat 'n' sassy smile, but yours was thin 'n' sassy, with that slender assy-like, well, how can I say it? A thin 'n' sassy smile on an almost wan face. Wan two, a buck and she's shoe. Three or four, I wish it were more. Five six? Pick-ups 'n' sex? Noo—not you—I think you'd rather get involved; though not exactly overwhelmed, not underwhelmed would do it either

Dressed in style, a swing and a smile—she came with a jingle, her hair in a mingle, a twingle and a trangle, and her threads in a tangle and tied like a bride of a laugh and a half, with the eyes of a sparkle, no signs of a darkle, with mirth and slim girth. She came with a clatter, no chatter but patter—her bright and her twyte, her lip all a pip, her giggle a-twiggle and laugh in a daft sort of way (let us bray)—hee haw and a squaw —not a teepee but try pie. Apple pie order—a geodesic dome, a bed of cut foam. "It's so neat in this dome, with a brush and comb here, and each stocking there and a mocking bird out *there*. (Time for a prayer?) Like you—and I *like* you. Life in a dome: can you cook? I'd be shook if you couldn't. And wouldn't you like a mouthful of stars on your head as you lie on your bed?

Sadie Mee—I saw her table and a sketch with a lable: "Self-Portrait." Sooo ex*press*ive (naw, Sue's her sister)—with one eye bigger than 'tother. Who could tether their pony—a stone pony of gin? Try agin! Who could tether her, feather her or weather her, whether her ups or her downs came through from the night—in the bright of the night? The bride of the night meets the king of the day (let us bray), while she stitches and sews on a curtain—a merkin of tangles and cloths at odd angles, the sun and the moon hint of purple bassoon sounds. Oh Sadie, mad lady of the autumn: slender bottom, mad ass of the lass with such class, whether glassy or grassy (not brittle though little)— I'd never be able to be still at your table. I'd wish with a swish, or I'd wash with a swash—and I'd dash (but not clash) with a dish—but not squish your good things)—or hope to taste your softness with more mince than hints. Tangles and jangles of cloth without spangles, but with bangles of soughts that make jangles of oughts. What I'd want, what I'd . . . like . . . oh why rock the boat! You're much younger than I, you've a magical eye. You've got womanly skills and your style hints of frills and great thrills—in your heart of hearts, an art of arts. "Come," you said, "if you want to."

Such a sketch, such a pleasure—in bright October weather —I'd not pester the nester of nights and of dawnings with croonings and fawnings—oh, Sadie Mee, could you look at me tenderly? Well, I felt like a surpliced ass without class. But you? A hint of badness, a taste of madness. She dreamed of her drawing, and I dreamed of her—that Sadie's some lady! Made eagles on cloth, with a bird and a moth, and the sun and the moon— on the curtain! To be strung. To be hung. In my daughter's room. There. And I've a secret prayer, which I feel, and it's real—as she's real: that I feel. But secret it stays, although my mind strays. Now the dream is sewn and the moment's flown. Still, there are the curtains . . .

7 July, 1977
Barton, Vermont

Other books by Dick Higgins include—
as author
What Are Legends (1960)
Jefferson's Birthday/Postface (1964)
Towards the 1970's (1969)
foew&ombwhnw (1969)
Computers for the Arts (1970)
Die Fabelhafte Geträume von Taifun-Willi (1971)
amigo (1972)
A Book About Love & War & Death (1972)
The Ladder to the Moon (1973)
For Eugene in Germany (1973)
Le Petit Cirque au Fin du Monde (1973)
Spring Game (1973)
City With All the Angles (1974)
Modular Poems (1975)
classic plays (1976)
Legends & Fishnets (1976)
Cat Alley (1976)
The Epitaphs/Gli Epitaphi (1977)
everyone has sher favorite (his or hers) (1977)
George Herbert's Pattern Poems:
In Their Tradition (1977)
A Dialectic of Centuries: Notes Towards a Theory of
the New Arts (1978)
The Epickall Quest of the Brothers Dichtung
and Other Outrages (1978)
I Colori/The Colors (1979)
as editor (with Wolf Vostell)
Fantastic Architecture (1971)
as translator
Hymns to the Night, by Novalis (1978)

750 copies of *some recent snowflakes (and other things)*
have been printed, of which 50 copies were bound in
cloth, signed and numbered.

this book was set in monotype bembo, a typeface de-
signed in 1929 by stanley morison and named for
cardinal bembo, a great patron of literature
and of fine printing in the 16th century.
the paper is mohawk superfine. type-
setting, printing & binding were
done by the stinehour press
of lunenburg, vermont
in the summer
of 1979.